Come Again into the World of Rod McKuen. A World Like Yours...

full of love, laughter, and tears, of well-remembered places and faces, of fleeting moments of the heart's unbridled joy, of shared silences and lonely longings . . . where the deepest feelings are born, and live on and on in the memory. . . .

". . . a man who has not only understood freedom for himself but for all the others for whom he writes and sings. The result is honesty—not just of his poetry, but of the man."

—Los Angeles Herald-Examiner

Love's been good to me

Rod McKuen

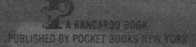

A KANGAROO BOOK
PUBLISHED BY POCKET BOOKS NEW YORK

A Biplane Book

Another *Original* publication of POCKET BOOKS

POCKET BOOKS, a Simon & Schuster division of
GULF & WESTERN CORPORATION
1230 Avenue of the Americas, New York, N.Y. 10020

Cover photograph by Wayne Massie © 1979 by
Montcalm Productions, Inc.
Photography by Rod McKuen
Photographs of Mr. McKuen by Wayne Massie and Hy Fujita

In addition to the books listed in the Sources section, some of the
poems in this collection have appeared in *The New York Times*,
Folio, *Woman's Day*, *Saturday Review*, *The Christian Science Mon-
itor*, *The London Daily Express*, *T.V. Times*, *Poetry Review* and
The Manchester Guardian.

ISBN: 0-671-82266-7

First Pocket Books printing April, 1979

10 9 8 7 6 5 4 3 2 1

Trademarks registered in the United States and other countries.

Interior design by Sofia Grunfeld

Printed in the U.S.A.

This book is for Wade
Alexander, my manager
and friend . . . . who,
traveling around the
world with me, seldom
makes judgements as
to my conduct.

Books by Rod McKuen

Prose
Finding My Father

Poetry
And Autumn Came
Stanyan Street & Other Sorrows
Listen to the Warm
Lonesome Cities
In Someone's Shadow
Caught in the Quiet
Fields of Wonder
And to Each Season
Come to Me in Silence
Moment to Moment
Celebrations of the Heart
Beyond the Boardwalk
The Sea Around Me
Coming Close to the Earth
*We Touch the Sky

Collected Poems
Twelve Years of Christmas
A Man Alone
With Love . . .
The Carols of Christmas
Seasons in the Sun
Alone
*The Rod McKuen Omnibus
Hand in Hand
*The Works of Rod McKuen
Love's Been Good to Me

*Available only in Great Britain.

Collected Lyrics
New Ballads
Pastorale
The Songs of Rod McKuen
Grand Tour

Music Collections
The Annotated Rod McKuen Song Book
The McKuen/Sinatra Song Book
New Ballads
At Carnegie Hall
McKuen/Brel: Collaboration
28 Greatest Hits
Jean and Other Nice Things
McKuen Country
New European Windows
Greatest Hits, Vol. I
Greatest Hits, Vol. II
Children's Song Book

Classical Music
Concerto for Cello & Orchestra
Symphony #1
The Plains of My Country
Six Piano Studies
The City
Concerto for Piano & Orchestra
Symphony #3

Opera
The Black Eagle

Contents

UP FROM THE STREETS

LITTLE TOWNS & PRETTY PLACES

AND IN THE COUNTRY

OTHER WORLDS

SIMPLE GIFTS

AND AFTER TOMORROW

Author's Note

LOVE'S BEEN GOOD TO ME is not a very extraordinary title for a collection of my poetry. I write about love often, in all of its aspects. If, in life, the feelings I've been willing to share have not always been greeted with the same amount of ardour I directed toward a love object I can't complain.

I've known certain minutes of pleasure worth millenniums of pain. And I assure you I was younger—perhaps a lot younger—when I stated 'there is no loving without losing.' I would amend that statement now and say that I have never loved and not learned something valuable . . . however difficult the circumstance, however lean the pickings, I always came away with more than what I gave. Even when I was sure I'd given the lot.

If there is a so-called *lot* (all there is) to loving, I'm convinced that several lifetimes would not, could not, exhaust the lover. If certain experiences I write about seem born of pain, they surely were, but the compensation—not always evident at the time, overrides the sorrow and self-pity.

Perhaps my banner with its strange device is merely made of hope heaped high on hope in the name of self-preservation. I don't think so. I enter into each relationship with trust and I am not easily convinced that something I want badly enough or believe in will not work. Love works if you work at it.

So much for platitudes, except that I'm convinced there is little life without love. Love has in common with living, good times—bad times.

Some years ago I wrote a song called LOVE'S BEEN GOOD TO ME. It was all about traveling and loving in different climates. This book is a collection of things I've written about the different climates of love. Some of the poems date back more than twenty years and were written in twice that many countries and places. Some of the poetry included here was selected with the help of friends. Good friends. Most of it was reselected in the middle of the night when friends are fast asleep and the written word is more a rival than a roommate. The newest poems were composed in Los Angeles and New York.

For as long as I can remember giving concerts I've stated at the end of each one "it doesn't matter who you love or how you love but that you love," adding, "If you came with somebody . . . be nice to them, if you didn't—look around." Last night in Philadelphia, after the second show, I forgot to remind the audience of that belief. And you know what, I came home alone.

R.M.
January 1, 1979
New York City

OF SONGS AND CITIES

Towns ring in the mind
like tunes of glory.
Cities hover over hearts
like mantles of gray sadness,
finally bluring—
in the afternoon and afterthought

Love's Been Good to Me
(The Song)

I have been a rover
I have walked alone
Hiked a hundred highways
Never found a home
Still and all I'm happy
The reason is, you see
Once in a while along the way
Love's been good to me

There was a girl in Denver
Before the summer storm
Oh, her eyes were tender
Oh, her arms were warm
And she could smile away the thunder
Kiss away the rain
And even though she's gone away
You won't hear me complain

There was a girl in Portland
Before the winter chill
We used to go a-courting
Along October Hill
And she could laugh away the dark clouds
Cry away the snow
It seems like only yesterday
As down the road I go

There was a girl in Houston
Out where the hot wind blows
Why I had to leave her
The God almighty knows
She could take
The long hot summer
And cool it with a sigh
But words have no more wisdom
When it's time to say goodbye

Words & music
Rod McKuen/1960

Of Songs and Cities

I live beyond the reach
of my own self sometimes,
                    outside of me.
Beyond the days
that chased me
down the summer beach.
Closer to the night
but not a part of it.
I am moved by others
and the schedules
that they've set for me
rather than my own watch.

That's all right.
I have always been a driven man.
The difference now
is that more often I'm a passenger,
instead of he who turns the wheel
                     and drives.

My battered sneakers
have carried me down streets
I may never walk again,
through towns I can't remember.
I've kicked them under beds
in musty rooms
and worn them on the gravel
of a castle courtyard turn-around.

Coming off a stage one day
I heard a lady whisper to her friend:
He's making money now,
surely he can afford a better kind of shoe.
Ah, but that's the thing—
money's earned for comfort's sake.
I'm comfortable in old things
with so much newness
working through my life.

I'm asked for wisdom sometimes, too.
Whatever love or message that I have to give
is woven in the texture of my poems and my songs—
          plain though they may be.
When all the schedules
have been met
and I'm alone again
new songs and parts of those
who've grown
and gone off
on their own
come rushing in;
demanding to be held
or asking if they
might be lent or given.

What I do
and give away
I do with love
there isn't any other way,
or if there was
I wouldn't use it.
Believe that,
for the only lies
I tell these days
are those I tell
about myself.

TAMING THE WILD HEART

Some still arm themselves
with whip and chair
as they set out across the lea
to tame the wild heart.
But only those who've yet to learn
that gentleness calms both,
the lover and the lion

Thirty-two

Smiles
are passports
through the desert
and visas to
all alien countries.

I am your family
and your winter fire
let me do your crying
and you can make
my smiles for me.

For S. C.

I do not know
what is more beautiful
than your tangled black hair
on a white pillow.
I have thought about it all afternoon
and decided not even butterflies or children
or the blossoms in the hills above the beach
can compare.

If I had money
I would not buy a comb or a red ribbon
to decorate it.

Instead I might charter worlds
so you could walk in them
and everyone could see your hair.

Missed Meeting

Odd we didn't meet
exchanging glances.
Falling down together
then fidgeting and fumbling,
coming together
on the Salisbury Plain.

Did I tell you
that I saw
        the Concord
            there?

Five
    six
or was it seven
            years ago
parked in a field
            and guarded,
back from nearly mastered
        maiden flights.

We might have met there
    earlier and easier.
It might have worked
where now it only hopes
and prays to work.

I know
that you were there then
training to be you
not necessarily the you
that I know now,
but the you
    you wanted.

Admission

Crawl with me
        through dawn
starting early.
So that we might do
                everything
there is to do.
Don't be the first
to go to sleep
or if you do
let me fall asleep
        inside you.
Let me hibernate
like a chipmunk
        or a bear
in the middle winter.

Inner Workings

I have seen you
when your smiles and frowns
were so tied up and intermingled
that none—not even you
could have said
with any sureness
what face you were giving
          to the crowd.

I have walked with you to subways,
then twenty minutes later
I have been with someone else
and never loved you less.

I have spied on you
and looked accusingly,
when I, myself, knew well
that I was in the wrong.

I have wept for you,
                    about you
and one time with you.
I have shared your secrets
and kept private
secrets of my own.

I have fought with you
and over you,
loved you and disliked you
in equal parts
and at the same time.

I have thought
that I would die
if you failed to turn up
on some pre-selected night
and when you didn't—
    wished I would.

I have loved you
never asking if I should.
I have trusted you
not caring if I could
        or couldn't.

In company
with strangers or your friends
I have smiled and gone on smiling
when I thought no single smile
                              or grin
was yet left inside me.

If we were unhappy
with one the other
why shouldn't it be
just our concern?

I have watched you play
with other people's children
and felt they were our own.

I've heard you hum
some made-up tune at breakfast
and watched you killing time all day
while you awaited killing me at night.

I have lied to you
for no good reason.
I have troubled you
and even when I knew it
sometimes that didn't make me stop.

The things we do
in love's name
never stop surprising me.
I'm amazed that love
can live at all
through all the subterfuge,
pass through all the barricades,
stumble over all the obstacles
we construct and put up
            in its way.

That first seed
wherever planted
must have been a hearty strain.

Just now
what kind of passion
stirs inside me
I cannot say.
I feel for you
and it's as much as love
but whether it's because
I feel you leaving,
slipping from me day by day
or because I need, depend on,
                    want just you
I have no way of knowing.

```
                    32 EMP        MDSE              CA
            8222460                            2.50+*
                     52U2                      2.50+S
                       4.000% TAX               .10+
      3040           52U2                      2.60+S
      3040           52U2                      2.60+T
      3040
                     5 18 79

      B Dalton
```

Our lives together
have become so knotted,
                    muddled up
that who's to say
            where the heart ended
and habit started in to open up?

I love you—yes
But I don't mean for you
                    to know it.

Celebration

Your feet came
noisily up the stairs
your eyes and arms
came bounding through the door
I stood there looking at you
too stunned to believe it true
too happy to disbelieve.

You came home.
I thanked God
a thousand times tonight.
Each time I touched you
I thanked God.

Eleven

You said
I'll always be there
and you are.

Sometimes
the distance
that you keep
is as difficult
for me to bear
as proximity would be
to anyone I didn't care for.

No Whisky Bars

I believe that crawling into you
is going back into myself.
That by the act of
joining hands with you
I become more of me.

There are no whisky bars
for dancers like ourselves,
and so we move into each other
like drunkards into open doorways.

My need for you is near addiction.

No sailor ever had tattoos
growing on his forearm
the way your smile
has willed itself back behind my eyes.

It will not dissolve.
It will not divide.
For I am nothing if not you.

WITHIN MIDNIGHT

Inside the midnight
we all know
I suspect another lurks
more beautiful
and with a closer moon.

§ 49

Nocturne

At twilight
spires pierce the middle air
as if to feel their way
through clouds and into
Gods green garden
and protected grass.

Later when the midnight comes
they venture further
perhaps into his living space.
I wonder how he greets
these round, well meaning domes
with pleasure or indifference.

Depending on his boredom
or the baccannle
of cheribim and serephim
                    in progress

I expect he welcomes
all the brave intruders
especially if their curiosity
is gently mixed with love

Midnights'
not as desperate
as we're told
we should believe it is.

Loving and the act of love
is only one more affirmation
that God in heaven
walks and runs
            and summersalts
living on to see
all things his hands created
die, arise and live again.

Eldon, Two

Your jealousy
below the colored lights
did not displease me.
Unwarranted or not
it said in silence
        those words
we should not say aloud
                just yet.

You honor me
with your attention,
your jealousy has made me proud.

Most of all
I confess that my existence
only comes from
                loving you.
Were it not so
I don't know
where my head would be.
In the meat rack
or on the chopping block
                I suspect.

Reintroduction

You're here.

Seeing you
the second time
makes me feel
I had my eyes closed
when we met before.

Yes
the *whole* of it
would be the best.
All pretense
not pretended any more.

But you are here.
That is enough for you
and by necessity for now
      enough for me.

      You're here.
What happens in this moment,
even if it's nothing,
      is enough.

Lesson: One

I leave you on the bed
still within the dark
       genuinely sorry
     that it came to this.
And then the long walk home
and climbing the stairs
to be alone
       and maybe sleep,
   or whatever,
but not to think.

The year twenty gone
I concentrate on twenty-one
and so begin to wonder
                    when it is
a man becomes a man.
Will I be officially informed
by the tax man or the rule book maker?

I've noticed that the hair
upon my belly's darkened
and it moves toward my chest,
yet though a forest stands
where only trees once stood
            I don't feel different.

I leave you
         walk away
sorry for the first time.

Tomorrow when you waken
there'll be sun
and you'll forget.
But me,
think how it is for me
not knowing what
the transformation means
or if it's come or will come.

I left you silent in the dark
but I know darkness too.

Excelsior

I celebrate your eyes
because they looked at me
without restraint or shame

I celebrate your breasts
in the darkest night
I could find them blind
              and feeble.

I celebrate your tears
even if they cry for something
            that I've done.

I celebrate you
playing shuffleboard
            or tennis
or playing with my balls
while I sleep.

I celebrate
all the night sounds
that you make
but won't admit to
your conversations with yourself
                    in sleep.

Most of all
I celebrate the god
that gave me you
and asked for nothing
in return.

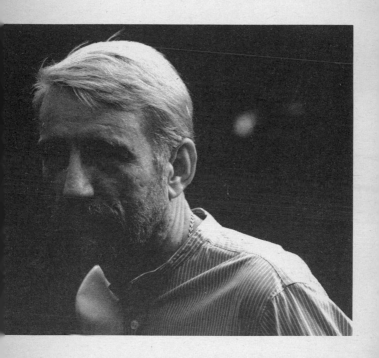

Mardi Gras

A Mardi Gras
is running riot in my head
made of goats on Spanish hills
whitewashed houses seen from trains
and bulls that run down pastures
still not green.

A Mardi Gras made of noise
and Christian names
not given and not learned
at the unmasking.

Whether I'm confetti killed
or thumped to death by noise
I ask that you believe
I wear no favor hat
           or mask
when I come chasing after you.

Love I wear
As open as a wound,
a mad mistake I know
but love, like Lent,
only comes to those of us
who still believe.

In loving
the only banner we can hoist
is love itself.

Excelsior!
I take this hill—
but with a white flag only.

You may tear my life
but not my flag.

The Coming of the Rain

It seems as though
the rain has not begun
and yet that it will never stop.

So much love has passed between us
that we've made the afternoon
last through half the night
by moving back and forth
            across each other
again and time again.

I'd love to fill you to the brim
so that you'd be always full
                    and spilling over,
then I could know for sure
no interloper however tall
weaving through the distance
would find shelter in you
from the next November rain
or hide your body
from the long
September shadows
          with his own.

And still it rains
as though the sky's let go
                    for always.
A thoughtful rain
as I go back to bed
and you go off
to make a chocolate cake.
The rain that I had damned
                    all morning,
I bless tonight.
Don't wake me if I fall asleep
even if your fist
          is full of frosting.

UP FROM THE STREET

Over my shoulder
what I have seen
is more important
than *now* to me.

ᓚᕬ *71*

Up from the Street

Safety seizes me
more often
as the years go by.
I stay at home
comfortable
with my discomfort
Sure because of my unsureness.

Silence owns me,
will not let me go
unless I force myself
out the door—
(now double-locked)
into the elevator
and out upon the street.

The street is beautiful.
Where once I kept
within the shadow
of tall buildings
I now parade in sunlight,
windowshop and stop
          for crossings.

Sometimes even greet
                old friends
I never knew had moved
into the neighborhood.

Once I'm on the street
I might meander
two blocks, five
          or anywhere.

If I pack a lunch
I might stay within the city
sunrise to the day's end.
but I'd remain on guard
showing off my sanity
making sure that passersby
continue in their passing
and so such preconceived a plan
as lunches paper bagged
and ready to be shared
is an indulgence
I cannot afford.

I might as well be home,
trimming sideburns, changing shirts
or studying my own reflection
            at the mirror's edge
(long ago I learned to shave,
tie ties and comb my hair
without confronting mirrors squarely.

The street exists for me
as a place of observation.
The pace I practice,
head down striding, straight ahead
is meant to preclude others
　　　　from observing me.

I will not say that dark intentions
fail to lurk inside of me
nor that I keep them in control
and they cannot of themselves
bob freely to the surface
but my forays are not so planned
that I darn undarned underwear
in case the truck or trailor's
　　　　aim is true
and I'm unmasked forever
by nurse or undertaker.

I am not afraid of streets
no alleyway has been
                antagonistic to me.
Highways leading east and west
and all the other variations
have been home.

But my new home is safety.
Not Rome or Omaha or
                    Oakland,
Paris or the scattered islands
pretending to be Greek.
While I bear no grudge
to Alamo or San Francisco,
their knives are sharpened
waiting not behind the structures
but in the naked or
the peopled paths for me.

But pride or paranoia
does not, will not
keep me from appointed avenues.
What I feel for sidewalks
is akin to how I loved
the railroad right of way
when I was ten and younger.

Perhaps I've run too often
in these so different
                    places
not to know
that what I feel
is more than dreaming.

I am not complaining.
City streets and those
            in little towns
have given me so much
that I could build
an airfield or a pyramid
out of all the outside
            spaces
I've been allowed to occupy.

Rejection, then, runs riot.
Perhaps I'm streetwise
        knowing that.
And while rejection
never seems to walk
        toward me
arms spread wide
and smile curled down.
It always waits
in Eastern cities.
That's the game,
taking the chance
looking rejection
        in the eye.
Curiously I'm never suspect
        of acceptance.
That has more to do with need
        than ego.

I need,
but I am not complaining
that would be disservice
to the worlds I've toured and traveled.

Even now,
despite the worry
that I cannot measure up
to what I think I should be
I know a new acquaintance,
friend and maybe more
will seek me out and find me.
If ever I forget
I've but to think back
to a nearby yesterday
to know that I've been rediscovered
nightly and twice nightly.
Just when finally sure
that I'd been relegated
to the backroom
and the field beyond the clearing.

This winter
after some deliberation
I've decided yet again
to give New York another try.

Those years ago on fifty-fifth street
when I sold blood and sometimes me
                    to keep alive
are not remembered sadly.
They were only different years
full of other kinds of circumstance.

I could count on Sloopy
when the world was turning
but not fast enough
now the needs not filled by others
have been assumed by Nickoli,
who sleeps just underneath my chin
and in the morning purrs me wide awake.

These days
my voice calls out
from too wide t.v. screens
exorting others to give blood
and in the space I've traveled,
(one block over to the right)
within the intervening years
I've been bought and sold
          electronically by experts

Surprisingly
a thirty-fifth floor penthouse
isn't that much different
from a three flight walk-up.
More public in the elevator, yes
but all my walls are thick.

Best of all
the New York City streets
are little changed
and more a home to me
than stereo and stainless chairs.

Do not be surprised
to see me then
breaking all the rules
I've here set down.
I'll get through the winter
               yes I will
bare headed and all smiles
even if I do so
step by step on city streets alone.
Crossing crossings
        or waiting for the light
                      to change
I go on hearing optimistic voices.

Could I
I would not deny
that even in this city's
                coldest cold,
its poorest gray mid-winter night . . .
almost more than anywhere,
once in a while along the way
love's been good to me.

Initial Encounter

The wind surrounding us
whistling, pounding
sounding like no wind
        ever sounded.

Safely
we rode out the night
        together.
When the sunlight came
you hid us both
  behind a pillow.

That first night behind us
a week now gone
a new one coming
you hide me still.
I am safe and sleepy
smiling, unafraid
ready to go forward
not walking, running
through all the storms
and all the sunshine
                    up ahead.

Night Piece

The lovers / hurry home now
to shut their doors
the sailors pair off
with the little boys
and the fat old women
and you and I are left alone.
The policeman walks on
through the fog
pacing
unaware
endlessly pacing.

everybody's star is falling
and clouds make patterns
on the ocean.

we will go home too
and finally with the liquor gone
the need for sleep forgotten
we will move together
and forget
the cruel suburban heat.
a star falls
and the world
is black and white again.

Sleep After
the Brighton Lanes

Saturday night
ducking, dodging
through the Brighton lanes,
pursuing and pursued.

When nothing comes
of conquest or conquistador
the quietude of that same
upstairs room
is like an iron mantle
clamping down and making
every organ useless.

And still sleep doesn't come.

It's then you know
that speech is nothing.
                    Not because
there is no one to speak to
but because yet one more time
you were not chosen
by the chosen
and you did not choose
                    to speak
even though the other
might have waited
thinking your words
should come first.

Why do we study,
why do we become
        learned men?
Why do we cheat
            and force
and push our way
through what we think
are fences
when all the while
it is those same
blind barricades
that we're erecting?

When it comes to *need*
intellect could not be
                more useless
and there's not knowledge
near enough or deep enough
to satisfy or substitute.

With imagination so well worn
that a single sigh is every bit
as powerful as sublimation.
Need can drive you
down the darkest alley
and leave you there,
beached and bloody,
still waiting for
the new encounter.

Need,
and need not gratified
has helped me understand
why the suicide can do it
and how the alcoholic can
transcend and thereby end
                    his limit.

Monday morning,
out of sleep,
too little sleep
that came too late.
The car is waiting.
On to Bournemouth.

Another night of faces
not seen completely
        and not seen again.
There are eyes and forms
that stand out even in the dark.
They become then individuals
                not audience.
They never know
and I can't tell them.

But should I put the question
to some of those who linger
when the show shuts down
and the answer came back *no,*
                what then?

One more bed
in one more room
now sleep hurries in,
even though the senses
still stay poised
for the small
or great adventure.
Tomorrow there's
the London train,
a month to go
and then
Los Angeles again.

Los Angeles

To love it
you have to understand
it's not a city
but an idea,
      whose time
is on its way and coming.

It helps to realize
these hamlets clustered
           here
are not in envy
of each other.

Brentwood
doesn't want to be the Beach.
The Valley's not in awe
of Holmby Hills.
Hollywood has no desire
to be North Hollywood
or East L.A.
Silverlake and Westwood,
miles apart
are content to be so.
Santa Monica Boulevard
the Canyons of Benedict
and Coldwater co-exist.

More people choose
to live inside these
                county lines
than were born
or will be born here.
Each has a different *why*.
Some prefer the openness
they think they've found
others like the being close
this place affords.

You will even find
a resident of forty years
who's catalogued a list
of disadvantages three pages long
that make the town unlivable.

He still lives here
and his catalogue
keeps growing.

Some feel trapped
while living in this
    unwalled place,
others say that here
they find existence
not a living space.

Every New Year's day
I pray for rain
so that Rose Bowl watchers
in the other thousand places
will be discouraged
from packing up
and moving here.

To love a city
such as this
means to try to keep it
private for yourself.
Maybe that's the reason
almost no one
wears the city's heart
upon their sleeve.

Sssh don't advertise.
Those disgruntled citizens
of Boston and Atlanta
have big ears.

Fun Raiser

I hate it all.
The dim light.
The forced smiles.
The long line
of literary bastards
sitting in quiet formation
on a never-ending couch
each looking like a personal
in the Saturday Review.

The now full
now empty martini glass
each with a delicatessen
                    toothpick
and a delicatessen olive.

All the men eyeing you
wondering
what we do at home.

Are there
any ways left
to tell you
that I love you
when the sum total
        is announced
when the final
word-count is made
from the last paragraph
                written
and the last word
            spoken
will I have said it all?

Come home.

Channing Way, 2

I should have told you
that love is more
      than being warm in bed.
                      More
than individuals seeking an accomplice.
Even more than wanting to share.

I could have said
that love at best is giving what you need to get.

But it was raining
and we had no place to go
and riding through the streets in a cab
                      I remembered
that words are only necessary after love has gone.

Out Beyond the Window
(Gstaad)

My window looks out over the park
Every year I've moved another story up
'Til now I'm almost close enough
to the roof of the sky to touch it.

I could even move the clouds aside
But no clouds come.
If they did, I'd welcome them
For I have few visitors here anymore.

Thirty

So close upon a narrow bed
that we are indivisible
I blot out everything
but your brown eyes.

And with the safety valve
of you at home
I last a single hour
in the marketplace.

LITTLE TOWNS &
PRETTY PLACES

If in the alphabet
you come upon words
you fail to understand
leave them awhile.

ـ§ *107*

Sunday One

I have no doubt
that Indian paintbrush
flower on the Colorado hills
all spring and summer long.
And these same aspen
lifeless now and leafless
in the cool pre-winter
could not I know
have been as beautiful
rouged and rainbowed
as they were
in last week's autumn.

Knowing this October day
will not repeat itself
we roll a while longer
on the cold damp earth
a mile above Georgetown.
Reckless in an open field
seen by anyone
savoring this same Sunday
in this same Sunday place.
Innocent we are
but not to any eyes
              but ours.

Good Sam
goes plodding through
the brush ahead
not noticing
    but taking notice
only just enough
to give us the horizon's edge
as he moves down into a gully,
not looking back
but pretending to be
plotting out or plodding down
     a new path.

Now eye to eye
and heavy-lidded,
till you force a smile from me
that crumples up the silence.

One more breath from you
                against my own
might have brought
a loss of innocence
giving us a gain of greatness.

I hope I never smile again
for after coming up
through almost forty years
I was but a breath away
from new breath
and new life.
But innocent I am
and will remain
of your body melting
                into mine.

Why you stopped the lightning
                  I can't say,
but Sam as he returned
careful to make noise
amid the underbrush,
and thus be heard,
looked as though
he'd tasted thunder.

Prisoner Beyond the Trees

I meant, I mean
to take you to the trees
or the tree country—
as I have planned consistently
to push you beachward.

The trees,
the seashores wait
while I lie next to you
in bed and wonder
will the trees
be tall enough
    to suit you?

The beaches
wide enough and sandy?
The cliffs along the coastline
as beautiful as those
you're used to
on your home-ground
                    outings?

Beyond the obvious
I have no reasons
as to why you've seen
so little of the
            California coast
each time you travel here.

I am not ashamed
to show you off
to anyone and all—
                I glory.
seeing your reflection
coming back to me
from other people's eyes.

What then?
Why keep you prisoner?
It could be I indulge myself
by letting only my eyes
                see you.
It must feel strange
to be a guarded guest.

Give me time
to take your face
                for granted.
I'm learning.

Manhattan Beach

I've taken a house at Manhattan Beach
working the summer into a book.

Eddie came last weekend
and brought two girls and some books.
The girls were pretty but the books stayed longer
and now they menace me stacked up on the floor
          staring back in unread smugness.

Otherwise I've had no visitors.

It's hard to sleep
though I try breathing with the waves.
It only makes me think
of our own breathing counterpoint.

At first I missed the traffic
    then the telephone.

Finally I call back
a hundred more familiar rooms
and sink down past the pillow's eye.
It's made me think I ought to try and buy
songs and safe surroundings I know best
and keep them in a half-packed suitcase
for sojourns such as these.

Katie keeps me company
and from her daily runs along the beach
brings me back fantastic things.
A weathered stick
              a bottle with no note
                        assorted other dogs.
She has, I fear, bad taste in canine friends
(the kind you say I've lately had in people).

Still lying by my bed at night
she smells like all the seas I've known
and that's a comfort to the sailor in me.

Will I see Capri again?
Hydra's just a name now
though once the big boats
        filled the harbor
and young Greeks made me dance,
while up above the Suco-Suco
a boy of fifteen stretched himself
and caught me thinking ten years back
regretting not the gone-forever mornings
but wondering only how I'd live
        another afternoon.

I nearly died that August.
Some fever made of lamb no doubt
or nightly walks along the harbor.
I stayed alive on summer squash and Coca-Cola
and wrote no songs.

No letters came that summer either
and I was down to eighty drachma
when I left the island.

Still I would go back
but not to Athens with its tear gas for the masses
and bayonets—
the buckshot of the upper classes.

Naples is the asshole of the world
        (ah, but there's Capri).
Majorca still has buggy rides
that take you to the sea.

Outside Katie's barking on the beach.
She's found a seal
            that wants to play.

Cannes

Cannes waking
in the winter morning
blue jackets sweeping down
the palm-lined street
and the empty bottles going back
to the empty-bottle places.

As jackhammers
do crossword puzzles
            on the sidewalk
and acrobats on painted yellow cranes
scoop out a new foundation
the stray cats crawl back under buildings
                    to avoid the noise.

Jet time zones
still adjusting in our heads
we mix the shoes up
in the hotel hallway
and lose another day
by going back to bed,
thanking God for January mornings
          and café crème
along the coasts of France.

Oak Harbor

Everywhere
oak harbor is awakening
                    to spring
the hills flower green
and dark green
the sky promises April
and the killdeer birds
always last to notice spring
begin their early march
across the meadow.

Today I left the island
the ferry boat
muscled away from the beach
for the last time
and I started
my journey home
imagining you still looking
at Mount Baker
from your second-story window
or polishing your skiis . . .
contemplating Colorado.

Fish Kites

We'll go to Tachikawa for the weekend.
As we slip by the fields
a hundred shades of green
run along the window of the train.

Boys' Day
and all the fish kites
will be flying from the rooftops.

Sink down into my lap and sleep.
Untroubled sleep of those who know
that weekends only last two days
and have an address list
of long-forgotten names
to prove it.

Belcher Landing

These days I own
the whole wide ocean—
all the sea
that I can see and more.
Some people say
they are my friends.
It is not enough,
or at the very least too much.

There was a time
sometime ago
when I owned only
one small pond
or part of it—
the other part belonged
to my friend Don.

We'd go swimming
at Belcher Landing
Don and me.
Then through the grove
of cottonwoods
still bare-assed and hungry
we'd hunt wild berries
and fall among the fern
no longer wanting
letting the sun get on
with ripening us.
We grew
almost before each other's eyes.

Ponds and people grow apart,
new needs push us in new directions
or in no sure direction.

I own the ocean now—
but it is only one small ocean
compared to that one large pond.
Some time ago it was
at the start of one certain summer.
I wonder what became of Don,
Belcher Landing,
and I wonder what became of me?

Postscript

Someone sends me news of Don
He's well. Selling blue parrots
in an animal store.
Married. Working in the courts.

I wonder if he still enjoys
                        surprises
I must be sure to watch
                  his eyes
as I crowd past the crowds
in some morning courtroom
with my own hastily made up brief
to stand beside him
as he starts his argument
before the sternest judge

or should I enter
that exotic pet shop
dressed in less than briefs
ready for that ancient
                    swimming hole

At Belcher landing

AND IN THE COUNTRY

Country alphabets are easy
down-to-earth and dignified.
Confusion only seems to come
from caring too much
without taking care.

x

◄§ 139

September Saturday

The country's there
four square
       and waiting.
The drive is twenty minutes
       hardly more
even on the oldest road.

You might ask *the drive to where*
I'd tell you if I knew
Perhaps I mean
the drive, the coming over
         into you.

Hurry.
The country's there
four square and waiting.

The First Time

Beyond the trees
of what the world
        terms wilderness
there is a first time.
Not to be confused
with anything
that's yet to happen
or what has gone before.

It feels not merely more,
but all there must be
           all there is.

Skating on your smile
            each night,
I know that I am safe,
privileged beyond
whatever God there is
to watch with you
the man-made stars.

Away from you
I don't exist,
nothing's true
or even false.
I've no one
to dress up for
no reason
to leave home
or even share what's left to share.
It must be that the learning stops
now that I've learned to learn
                              with you.

Coming Close

I wanted so
to bend the bough
but never once
to break the branch.

I hoped
that I might see
the blossoms
     fall intact
without the petals
        coming loose
or even once detached.

What I wanted most
        was love
in a straight
straightforward way.

I wanted you
not as you could be
had I made you up
but the way I found you
no different from
the way you really are.

I thought by now
we might have earned
a chance to come down close
and lie against the earth.

But I'm convinced
the earth will not allow
even its truest lover
to belong to it
now or straight away.

I cannot care
a little for you.
I love you only just enough
to love you all the way.

Noon Again

Your thighs
are like a hidden
          honeycomb
as we move
closer now.

How is it that the bee
has left your legs
          untouched
surely he can smell
the sweetness
      waiting there.

I open them
        with pride
before the sun.
Spread them wider still
so that every ray
of sunlight catches them
drinks them in
as I will soon.

You rub your belly
like Italian women
kneading bread
as I move down
between your legs
        closer still
but not as close
as I will finally be
before the noon
        takes over.

Has clover
ever smelled as sweet
as your warm body
growing warmer still.

Slowly now
I'll be easy
but I want to fill you up
fuller than I've filled myself
with drink or eating.

Breast to breast
        then down
between your thighs
            once more
a sweet triangle
bringing certainty
into my life.

Don't move.
I'll make the motions
            wide enough
to take us both
beyond the sun
and back again
to focus on your eyes.

Vermont

However small this time
let me catch it
        in my teeth
holding it as it holds me
tightly and for now.

If the snow
runs faster than we planned
I'll hold on when you let go
and lead you back again
through that powdered
        Vermont snow.

Through the Autumn Field

Moths fill up the morning
and spiders slide down shafts
    of sunlight.
The wind now makes a long,
      slow moan.
Tired of all the old Octobers
the moan is more a sigh.
Resigned and lonely
      like those of us
  who face the wind
the wind itself on seeing autumn
      runs to hide.

I walked home
through the field
        alone
looking at the row on row
    of dead cornstalks
frightened by the frost
    arrested by
the first long breath of autumn.
Feeling a little older
but with no new knowledge.

Passing through
        the now past summer
I've learned nothing.

True, I've memorized your thighs
your burnt brown breasts
your eyes, your eyes
but you were busy memorizing
        other people's hands
the kindness
of their summer crotches
the sounding of their sighs.
Without attending
            your same school
as pupil or as teacher
I've become your *familiar*.

Autumn is a signpost
          for the leaving.
Whether leading us
to comfort or despair
autumn points the way.

Bend to me
this first long
autumn night
or let me bend to you.
Everything and nothing
has passed between us
and tomorrow
I'll pass by again
through frosted fields
where even pumpkins
now detach themselves
from dead and drying vines.

OTHER WORLDS

We need not journey
off to other planets
in order to find other worlds.
Planets that the heart
has trouble comprehending
sometimes sit across the street.

Winter People

Discarded. Given up.
with lifetimes left to give.
Life itself has been
their cloak and classroom
now sent away to live
or pretend at living
                not students
or the jailer children
who shuttled them
to ghettos of neglect
                come calling.

Now voyager, I ask you
did you do your early traveling
(turning from the spinster aunt
                to Cinderella)
                    for this?

I have seen them
in the winter,
sitting on the same
            long benches
(before they sit,
carefully dusting the snow
      from off the green
of those slatted sitting places.

No pidgeons left to feed,
All have made their winter
                        pilgrimage.
But tomorrows papers
being read today
because these so called
                  senior citizens)
(a tiny two word prison name)
are clairvoyant, every one.

Old man
how old is old?
one half of one ear
lost to hearing?

A smile that didn't
come on time
because you felt the need
to *think* before you acted
on a not so funny joke?

They put old people—
Sixty-five is just about the age—
in padded cells
     for less than that.

Old couples,
odd as obelisks
that really do inspire,
should fortune
or a child with fortune
            intervene
You might be interned
in some high rise museum
As proof of your true worth,
Within your childrens eyes.

Old friends of course,
Will still be in the neighborhood
You never wished to leave.

Don't depend on visits.
Your new familiars
will be families of every kind
appearing once a week on television.

Widows, widowers
and, those about to die
You've been given up
by those you gave to,
but I beg you
don't give up on your own selves.

Write. Wire. Call collect.
Anybody. Dial a prayer or me,
talk radio shows, the president.

Don't let go
especially if there is even
one relative poised and purring,
spoiling to collect the spoils.

Do not forget, rewrite your will
cutting out petition signers
and children busy during business hours
(business being anything but you).

Leave your estate
to the state, the city
          or the country
(they were always late—
but never too late)
or sign it over
to one of the few
who thought about you
never knowing you
but caring all the same.

I care about
the winter people,
love them as the lilacs
blooming still amid the snow—
but check me out
before you will to me
your lorgnette
          or your dusty bible,
as a lover, loving
when and where I can
I love true and truthfully
giving over all I own each time,
that would include your legacy.

Letter from Sydney

The letter finally came
Bushtail possum
        on the postage stamp
seven days from Sydney
                        to L.A.

No, six.
Moving past the dateline,
        it came today.

I would that I
were travelling back
with your letter's answer
carried on my tongue
                to yours.

I would look at you
in the easy winter night
of New South Wales
and you would know
that my urgency
for answers to unframed questions
comes from the necessity
of being with you,
not just the luxury or need.
You are a fact for me
            not dream or fiction.

I agree that time
will test us
but time not spent with you
                is lost.

For Bimby

Some things you cannot
put down in a new way.
Sheep grazing on the airport road
                            from Rome.
Stale February days and Bimby's smile.

Balloons never look like clouds to me
                or crackerjack surprises
or anything but just balloons.
So it is with Bimby's smile
held in the Roman day
ablaze with waking tourists
                            and sleeping cats
and ruins being ruined
                by the tick of time.

Her smile is just her own
                    without elaboration
lost in the Alitalia afternoon.

Sunrise

How is it sunrise
strikes a different chord
　　　　each day.

Soft one morning
loud and full of life
and self-importance
on the next.

I have ridden
off to work
with sunrises I remember
　　to this day
and sat upon the sand
greeting summer sun
　　　　on Sundays
when I had nothing else
　　　　　to do
no one else to sit
and talk and sing to.

God make the sunrise come today
but soft for I'm alone.
You needn't shout
for there'll be no one else
but me to hear.

Morning on the Chobe River

Fish eagles swoop,
miss their catch
and swoop again.
A hippo bobs up
        to the surface
then another
and yet a third
            like apples
in a party barrel.
Now the baboon family
            has arrived
swinging, scratching one another
marching in a row
        toward the waterhole.

I am waiting
for the giant of them all.
Far off
you can hear them
threading through the bush
their trunks trimming
all the leaves
from all the lowest branches
of all the trees they pass.

God must have looked at man
and then decided
he could do a better
         bigger job
make something *really* beautiful
and so before he stopped to rest
he made an elephant.

Some Silent Winter

How it must feel
to light the world
with bon-bon songs
and never weep again
in the darkness or the noon.

But sweet songs
come from covenants with God,
if you would sing sweetly
be sure the right God
catches you while walking
and when he turns you 'round
be sure he walks you safely
down the first half mile.

And now I love you
and I live you as well
because of you I am larger
                 than myself
I am as big as both of us
I live because I love you
I love because
there is you to live for
and you to love,
and falling asleep against you
or thinking I'm against you
is all the bon-bon song I need
to fill my world.

The Snows of Amsterdam

You can almost hear
the snow fall down
            in Amsterdam.
It comes with such a force
that people in the streets
bend forward weighted down
                  like trees.
They shield themselves
like frightened deer
ducking doorway to doorway
till they're safely home.

Diligently and evenly
the snow now covers
every street and sidewalk.
Nothing's left to chance,
              as slowly
through the near-deserted town
the clouds unlock their fists
and let the snow fall down.

The ground is now
all winter white
not Pendleton
but sheet white
        like a made-up bed.
The clouds have done their job.
But who's to say where God's cloud ends
and the snows of Amsterdam begin.

Corfu

Marilyn learned Latin
so that she could talk
intelligently to Greeks.
No, not talk,
confuse them
with *one-upmanship*
practiced on these islands
but called by many
different kinds of names.

Marilyn was masquerading
but she presumed
        that tourists
and the native too
who passed her table
in the Cafe Domas
were enthralled
intimidated and in awe
of such an intellectual.

An avocation
or a new vocation?
She never stopped
to think about it
or to wonder.

Marilyn was living now
        not existing
as she had been
all those years
in Starbuck Texas.

SIMPLE GIFTS

When the going's hard
the giving's easy . . .
don't hold back,
    give way

≤§ *189*

Another Thank You

Thank you for kissing me
in the elevator last night.

Holidays meant little
when I was young,
only supper at separate tables
from the grown-ups.

So thank you for the flowers
and the snow this morning
and for jam from the delicatessen
and for loving me.

Thank you for this one-room world.
    (All I need
           when you're here.)

Today while lying face to face
with love again
I closed my eyes to seasons and to skies
and I was younger than I've ever been.

                Thank you.

Christmas Past

I loved your face
on Christmas Eve,
though it was framed
by such a noisy crowd.
Seeing your eyes dance
and dance in my direction
was how I came to know you.

Seeing you beyond the tree
and only later on
     beyond my reach
was how I came to love you.

And if you loved my face
as much as you love Christmas,
I'd be safe from year to year.

The same anticipation
that you hold for holidays
    would smother me,
and glad I'd be to die so loved.

Art Piece

A statue
sometimes comes to life
without a wand
or mumbled magic.
Not muttered incantations
       or set prayers
will make it breathe.
You've but to love an object
       bronze or wooden
or molded plaster—
even paper eucalyptus trees
will finally breathe or wink,
at a certain moment
those who love
a work of art
will not be so amazed
to see the canvas
    or the cut-out
love him back.

Friday

How right to love you,
across the room
across the seas
and if need be
all across a lifetime
with you or without you.

Your going is a fact,
your taking leave
with but a telephoned goodbye
       almost a certainty.

I'll gain no understanding
from your absence
and any truth I fall upon
by my own hand
would have met me sooner
had you been beside me
to attract and guide it
down our double road.

Sunday Two

I wish for you
Sweet Sunday psalms
and carols of an evening,
sung out clear and strong,
coming up from chests
you haven't lain against just yet—
but will.

I wish you free,
face down in every lap that walked away
without your head pressed hard
against its Venus mound or crotch.

Surprising you midsentence
                    unsuspectingly
caring and carrying you carefully
to his own—your own Eden.

I wish you vintage wine
in every Coca-Cola glass

an end to wishing
signaling you've found forever
at the end of now.

Could I command your mouth
to talk at my ear only
and climb on my mouth every time
you know I would and more.

I'd wish beyond all reason.
Because I want
            beyond all want
                        for you.

Sunday Three

We cannot go both ways
though I know you'll try.
I could take you up one road
                and down another,
but one Sunday middle-month
is not enough to start a trip,
let alone do a journey justice.

So we meet and part
and maybe meet again,
lonesome travelers hiking
up some hill of hope
then down a Denver Sunday
at the summer's start.
I don't know where I am.
                Do you?

I would wish for you the world
if it were good enough for you,
each morning sky
                    hanging
                        out
                            there
                        clear as crystal.
I'd reel in for you
and doing so, make real.

AND AFTER TOMORROW

If it's Monday
I can think ahead to Wednesday
                    well almost
It surely would depend on how
last Friday came and went

Portland/June, 1978

It went so well
     in Portland,
So well, so long ago
I don't go back
that often, anymore
Why tempt the too long winter
to finally keep me there

Though that city
must have set the pace
for all the years to come
it holds longer in the head
that on the diary page

A letter once arrived
Postmark smudged
and no return address
but I could tell
From all the proper prose
and well spelled words
that it came from Oregon.

Did I remember. Yes.
Not embellished memory
but the way it surely was

There was a girl in Portland
before the winter chill
We used to go a-courting
along October Hill

Denver/October, 1978

Denver
little time to dance
and all the dance halls
       two feet wide
that rules one way out.

Walk, but where?
No roadmaps are provided.

Friends? All but one have moved,
but the citys arms stay open
you've only to loose weight
and slide inside.

One day, maybe.
One dark dependable
mile high day.
I'll get down again
            in Denver
and boogie country-style.
Not bumpings to
a Donna Summer whimper
but stomping as a fiddle
bows its way
through Cotten-Eyed Joe.

Still *there was a girl in Denver*
before the summer storm
Oh, her eyes were tender
Oh, her arms were warm

Houston/January, 1979

There was no girl
in Houston, this time.
Yes they were there
though rejection is not even
Strong enough a word
for how the gentle,
beautiful and finally lost
young ladies and a later
                    generation
made me feel.

But I have Texas memories
They go back
beyond the counting years.

Not just Dallas, Houston,
San Antonio or Fort Worth
but Galveston and Amarillo
even Magic City lives for me.
Each can help me back
to certain times,
merely by the mention
        of their names.

Yes *there was a girl in Houston*
Out where the hot wind blows
Why I had to leave her
the God Almighty knows . . .

I Am Heading Homeward

Arms full of promises
beds full of dreams
a head full of songs and none—
no one to hear them
at close quarters.

I am heading homeward
homeward bound am I
        traveling from
the farthest point north
        in California
to its middle and to home.

Having felt your strength
come into me
from the first long touch
to the last hand clasp
I am stronger now.

But I am weak from wanting,
tied up in knots from so much need,
wound in a ball and doubled over
from happenstance
that wouldn't,
    will not go on happening.
Stopped still am I
from your so fragile so firm hand.
You left me more a boy
        and less a man
than I might have cared to be.

Listen to me
I am finally going home
to double over and be sick
on my own ground
to weep my guts out
in my own back yard.

Leaving you was hard.
Your leaving harder.
I am going home to bear witness
to your having been with me
and some time up ahead
if I am living and still looking
I'll restock the larder
you left empty.

I am still together
heading home
          but not sure how.

Though we'll not meet again
I'll still be melding into you
                    and sweating,
standing next to you, unsteady,
facing you afraid for always.
Down the never-ending
                    middle nights
out and over all the days
that may be left to me.

Your leaving gave me
my own birthmark
like the clot inside
                    some feeble
and unbalanced head.
I wear it up above my heart
my own red badge of courage,
my own and only birthmark
          attesting to my birth
                    whenever.

I am heading homeward
        let me go.
The heart grows tired,
timid and afraid sometimes.
It needs to rest
as much as any head
on aching shoulders.

If I can go on
dreaming up safe seas
                and seaweed
my mind will still stay well,
but this old heart
grown older by its own mistakes
needs resting and a resting place.

Eldon, One

Maybe there are
no more doors
if this is so
I'm glad the last one
opened up on you.
Should I go on ahead
I'll leave a trail
of bread crumbs
or multi-colored twine
to help me find
the way back
to this happy place.

Having seen your eyes
I need no different
shades of green.

Don't Imagine Endings

It doesn't end here.
Here being where you are
or where you go and go again.

Please don't read belief
         especially my belief
               as mysticism
it's only that I know
you cannot work and wonder
and go on working
and end up with only
wrinkles on the outside
and inside warped images
of what could have been.

No trick or treats or magic
produce a heaven
or a proper hell.

Borrow? Yes.
Give back?
If your conscience
catches you in time.

Keep?
Not since they peopled pyramids
with bandaged bodies
soaked in henna leaves and oil
has one among us slipped away
and taken with them
anything of value.

But somethings out there,
if not on platforms
            or a cloud
somewhere, somehwere.

Why not believe?
The cost is negligible.
the truth of anything
not known, but certainly supposed
is not quite as sure
as anything we know.

What do we know?
Nothing anyone has yet
            been able
to prove or if so,
            improve.

Go to sleep with ease—
For hours or forever
as far as anybody knows
it could or could not be
your first step into heaven
or the last you take
leading *from* forever.

The Green

I'll survive, I will.
Whatever hill I'm asked
to climb or crawl upon
whatever dry space
I must travel through
to where the green
of this oncoming season
stays to speak to me,
I'll be there.

Wait for me
whoever you are.
Whatever tunic or bright shirt
                    you wear,
I'm coming, I'll be there.

About the Author

ROD McKUEN'S books of poetry have sold in excess of 17,000,000 copies in hardcover, making him the bestselling and most widely read poet of our times. In addition, he is the bestselling living author writing in any hardcover medium today. His poetry is taught and studied in schools, colleges, universities, and seminaries throughout the world.

The composer of nearly 2,000 songs, Mr. McKuen's works have been translated into Spanish, French, Dutch, German, Russian, Japanese, Czech, Chinese, Norwegian, Afrikaans, and Italian, among other languages. They account for the sale of nearly 200,000,000 records. His songs include "Jean," "Love's Been Good To Me," "The Importance Of The Rose," "Rock Gently," "Ally Ally Oxen Free," and several dozen songs written with the late French composer Jacques Brel, including "If You Go Away," "Come Jef," "Port Of Amsterdam," and "Seasons In The Sun." Both writers have termed their writing habits together as three distinct methods: collaboration, adaptation, and translation.

Rod McKuen's film music has twice been nominated for Motion Picture Academy Awards ("The Prime Of Miss Jean Brodie" and "A Boy Named Charlie Brown") and his classical work, including symphonies, concertos, piano sonatas, and his very popular "Adagio

For Harp and Strings" is performed by leading orchestras. In May, 1972, the London Royal Philharmonic premiered his Concerto No. 3 for Piano and Orchestra and a suite, "The Plains Of My Country." In 1973 the Louisville Orchestra commissioned Mr. McKuen to compose a suite for symphony orchestra and narrator, entitled "The City." It was premiered in Louisville and Danville, Kentucky, in October, 1973, and was subsequently nominated for a Pulitzer Prize in music. He has been commissioned by the city of Portsmouth, England, for a symphonic work to commemorate the sailing of the first ships from that city to Australia. The new work will be jointly premiered in Portsmouth and Australia's Sidney Opera House. (Mr. McKuen was the first American artist to perform a series of concerts during the opera house's opening season.)

His Symphony No. 3, commissioned by the Menninger Foundation in honor of their fiftieth anniversary, was premiered in 1975, in Topeka, Kansas, and he has appeared to sell-out houses with more than thirty American symphony orchestras. The author has completed the libretto and music for a full-length musical, *The Black Eagle*.

In July, 1976, two new McKuen works were premiered at St. Giles Church, Cripplegate, in the City of London. A Concerto for Cello and Orchestra and the first major symphonic composition written for synthesizer and symphony orchestra. (Concerto for Balloon and Orchestra.)

As a balloonist he has flown in the skies above the western United States and recently South Africa.

He likes outdoor sports and driving. Much of the author's time is now spent working for and with his nonprofit foundation Animal Concern and attempting to change laws in states and countries that allow public and private agencies to collect, but withhold, information from private citizens concerning their birth rights. Recently he has been active in attempting to ensure the passage of the Equal Rights Amendment and actively works to bring about human rights in all areas. He is a founding member of the First Amendment Society. In 1978 Rod McKuen received the Horatio Alger Award, was named by the University of Detroit for his humanitarian work and in Washington was presented the Carl Sandburg Award by the National Platform Association as, "the outstanding people's poet, because he has made poetry a part of so many people's lives in this country."

For nearly a year Mr. McKuen has taken a sabbatical from concerts and touring to work on the television documentary series, "The Unknown War," as poet, composer of the film's score and co-adapter, with producer Fred Weiner, of the scripts.

Having recently taken up residence in New York, the composer-poet now divides his time between Manhattan and the California Coast.

Sources

From the privately printed quarterly *Rod McKuen's Folio,* six poems have been chosen for inclusion here; "September Saturday," "Art Piece," "The Green," "Sunrise", "Morning" and "Mixed Meeting."

Come To Me In Silence was Mr. McKuen's second book for Simon & Schuster. Three of the poems first published there are in this collection; "Sunday Two," "Sunday Three" and "The Snows of Amsterdam".

And Autumn Came was originally published in diary form; as such, the entries had dates as headings. Here they have been given titles; August Third is "Night Piece," October Thirteenth "Fun Raiser," March Sixth "Oak Harbor" and February Fifteenth "Celebration."

"Inner Workings," "Reintroduction" and "Friday" are from *Moment To Moment.* "Vermont" and "Mardi Gras" first appeared in *Fields of Wonder.*

The first book of Mr. McKuen's trilogy using "the elements" as a canvas for his poetry is *The Sea Around Me,* the second *Coming Close to the Earth.* From the former "I Am Heading Homeward" was chosen, the latter provides "The First Time," "Noon Again," "Coming Close" and "Prisoner Beyond The Trees".

"Cannes," "Manhattan Beach," "For Bimby" and "Fish Kites" are from *Lonesome Cities*. "Channing Way, 2," and "For S. C." first appeared in *Stanyon Street & Other Sorrows*. "Thirty," "Thirty-two" and "Eleven" were taken from *Caught In The Quiet*.

From the first edition of *Celebrations Of The Heart* the author has excerpted "Belcher Landing," "Excelsior," "Some Silent Winter," "Admissions" "Letter From Sydney" and "Eldon Three" which has been retitled "Initial Encounter". "Eldon One & Two" are both from *Beyond The Boardwalk,* as is "Through the Autumn Field".

And To Each Season is the source for "Sleep After the Brighton Lanes," "Lesson: One" and "The Coming of the Rain".

"Out Beyond The Window" is from *A Man Alone*. "No Whiskey Bars," originally titled, "May 17th," was published in *In Someones Shadow*. "Thank You" is from *12 Years of Christmas* and *"Christmas Past"* is part of *The Carols of Christmas*.

Poetry written especially for this book includes "Up From The Street," "Houston/January 5, 1979," "Denver/October, 1978," "Portland/June, 1978," "Don't Imagine Endings," "Nocturne," "Los Angeles," "Postscript," "Corfu," "Winter People," a reworking of "Of Songs and Cities," and the couplets that open each section of the manuscript.

Index to First Lines

ROD McKUEN's *folio*
A UNIQUE EVENT IN PUBLISHING HISTORY!

Rod's private, unpublished poems and prose available for the first time in a quarterly journal. Each copy is signed and numbered and offered to subscribers on a very limited basis.

Some of the highlights featured in the past 20 issues include the only publication anywhere of Rod's Pulitzer Prize nominated prose/ poetry work THE CITY, his unpublished diary of travels through Europe, Russia, and South Africa, special holiday poetry and prose, McKuen Haiku poetry, very personal poetry for his son, and selections from his long-suppressed THE MORNING OF MY LIFE.

FOLIO always includes poems not previously published elsewhere . . . some appear in FOLIO long before later publication in other sources (and even then in drastically altered form).

FOLIO is published 4 times a year to benefit Animal Concern. Original charter subscriptions were limited to 1000 and have long been sold out. Issues are never sold individually. A LIMITED NUMBER OF NEW CHARTER SUBSCRIPTIONS ARE NOW BEING ACCEPTED AT $16.00 per year. FOLIO will continue to be a limited edition periodical and each copy will be illustrated by leading artists, numbered and personally signed by the author.

NOTE: new subscribers will receive as a bonus a free FOLIO box that holds up to 24 issues.

Enclosed is $_____

Please send me _____charter subscriptions to
ROD McKUEN'S "FOLIO" @ $16.00 for 1 year (4 issues)
Please send me _____copies of
ROD McKUEN'S "AND AUTUMN CAME" @ special price of $19.95

Name _____

Address _____

City _____ State _____

Country _____ Zip Code _____

Sorry, No C.O.D.'s/On orders outside the continental U.S., please add 50¢.
Calif. Residents add 6% sales tax. Make Checks Payable to:

CHEVAL/STANYAN CO.
Suite 1, 8440 Santa Monica Blvd., Los Angeles, CA 90069

THE GIFT FOR SOMEONE YOU LOVE
. . . MAYBE EVEN YOURSELF

AND AUTUMN CAME — ROD McKUEN'S
MOST ROMANTIC BOOK AND THE
LEGENDARY WORK THAT STARTED IT ALL!

Rod's first book of poetry, originally published in 1954 and for many years an unobtainable collector's item, AND AUTUMN CAME was reissued in 1969 in a special new deluxe edition — hand bound, boxed, numbered, and signed by the author in a *very* limited printing. Critics have hailed the work as a rare find and a key to understanding Rod McKuen's genesis and growth as a poet.

AND AUTUMN CAME is evocatively hand-lettered and illustrated with line drawings by one of America's most acclaimed artists, Anthony Goldschmidt. Reproduced on the same special paper created for Andrew Wyeth's watercolors, 12″ by 12″ and stamped in 24-karat gold, this deluxe book has won several international awards for its beauty and innovative creativity.

Originally offered for $50 at leading book and art stores, the first and only printing was sold-out. The only remaining copies come from Rod's private collection and are offered at a very special price to benefit Animal Concern.

AND AUTUMN CAME will *never* be reprinted, and to preserve the value of this edition for collectors — all original plates and proofs have been destroyed.

AND AUTUMN CAME is certainly the most unusual, distinctive, and touching book of poetry ever published.

The few remaining copies are available on a first-come, first-served basis only.

REGULAR PRICE: $50.00
SPECIAL PRICE (TO BENEFIT ANIMAL CONCERN): $19.95